Skateboarding: Rails, Rails, Rails

Written by
Evan Goodfellow

Photography by
Tadashi Yamaoda

Tricks performed by
Evan Goodfellow and friends

Skateboarding: Rails, Rails, Rails

Evan Goodfellow

Veva Skateboard Books Ltd.

I dedicate this book to my friends and family.
Thanks for your support.

Acknowledgements

Thanks to:

Tadashi Yamaoda: www.TadashiPhoto.com – Photography
Daryll Peirce: www.ArtDerailed.com – Art and Design
Matthew Gibualt - Main Editor
Trent Young – Assistant Editor

Canadian Skateboarders:

Steven Popp
Daniel Suppa
Mike Warkentin
John Ketsadachan
Jetski
Timmy Oberg

American Skateboarders:

Jeremy Reeves
Kellen James
Jake Smith
Tommy Sandoval
Steve McNeal
Brandon Turner
Mike McGowie
Ryan Nixs
Chris Troy
Jason Clary
Moses Salazar

Those who helped during the shooting:

Devin Komarniski, a.k.a Devo
Chris Kendall
Niall Conway

www.vevaskateboardbooks.com

Preface

Skateboarding is the best sport in the world because in comparison to other sports, you don't need much money, there are so many avenues of self-expression and you can always find new ways to challenge yourself. You can enjoy skateboarding by yourself or with friends. There is an overwhelming amount of diversity within the sport, ranging from street to ramps, and a combination of the two. You can push yourself to extremes or just cruise around and take it easy. You don't need any coaches or referees; instead, you need creativity and guts. The skateboarder is left to use the surrounding environment and imagination to try new tricks and develop one's ability.

Since skateboarding is so unscripted and free, and because it is a sport that welcomes progression, many individuals express a desire to learn new tricks that are beyond their understanding or ability. Some individuals wish there was more support to help learn new tricks, rather than just trying to figure them out on their own. This book is intended to provide the reader with a better understanding of how certain tricks are performed, along with the mechanics needed to better master one's skateboarding environment. Although this book focuses particularly on handrails and its ultimate aim is to help the skateboarder reach the next level, the tricks taught can also be applied to curbs. It should be understood at the beginning, however, that this book is intended for individuals with a more advanced ability.

Handrails are challenging because they require the skateboarder to maneuver with split-second precision. Handrails are typically thin bars high off the ground, and because they leave little room for error, they often lead to numerous falls and injuries. In addition, the fear factor often makes maneuvering even more difficult because the skateboarder has to deal with jittery legs and the fearful thoughts of worst-case scenarios. However, when fear is conquered and tricks are landed on a handrail, some of the most exhilarating feelings in the sport can be experienced.

In this book the photography and writing combine to paint a comprehensive description of what is required for each trick. Pictures alone are not enough. An individual can watch countless videos of professional skateboarders grinding and sliding rails, only to be confused and frustrated when, in a real-life situation, he or she tries to apply what was seen. In reality, to best learn a trick a written description is also necessary. A well-written description compliments pictures and helps the reader understand, point by point, the specifics of the trick (i.e., foot placement, weight distribution, and angle of approach). Consequently, the reader of this book will encounter a balanced combination of both words and pictures, everything necessary to master the grinding and sliding of both small and high rails. We hope that you enjoy the book and take away the knowledge needed to demolish the biggest, gnarliest rails you can find.

Warning Label:

Skateboarding is an extremely dangerous sport. Riders should wear safety equipment at all times and should not try anything that is dangerous or beyond their ability. Although riders in the book do not wear safety equipment, they are trained professionals.

Contents

Rail Tricks

Introduction

Growing up in central Canada and having to endure harsh winters can be torturous to the soul. However, when the snow melts in the spring, skateboarders are left feeling as if they have awakened from a decade long sleep and they are ready to skate with renewed passion and vigor. The melted snow leaves puddles all over the ground and bothersome traces of gravel. In the winter, the gravel is welcome: the city safety crews layer the icy roads with it to prevent car accidents. But in the spring it is a nuisance and skateboarders from around the city carry brooms to clean off the walkways and curbs so they can begin skating again. For me, this spring excitement has always been a vivid memory because it was in the spring that I grinded my first rail.

I remember that time of my life clearly. In the summer of 1996, Toy Machine skateboard company released the video "Welcome to Hell," which featured insane tricks being done on massive rails. The most memorable part in the video was Jamie Thomas' as he began his part doing two large rails back to back: the first was a backside lipslide, the second a backside 50-50 grind, and both were accompanied by the intensely stoking music of Iron Maiden. The video was a huge success and it created a worldwide desire in the hearts and minds of skateboarders to learn to master rails of all sizes—short, round, flat, large, long, and high.

After the video came out, my friends and I began practicing our basic tricks on curbs, such as 50-50's and 5-0's, so that we could take them to the next level, which were rails. Rails were a scary thought, often associated with the image of landing on one's testicles and afterwards peeing blood for a week. We were determined though, and set our minds on mastering the art of rail skating. Several friends had their fathers weld flat bars, and one friend even ran into a few stop signs with his mother's minivan to get the ultimate square rail. Although these flat rails and curbs were only basic, skating them daily helped us pave the way towards our ultimate goal: genuine handrails.

That winter we were fortunate when a local church allowed us to skateboard in its cement-floored gym, which was a giant cement room that had once been an old bowling alley. It proved to be the practice we needed to hone our rail skills. Every day we would leave high school and trudge through a snow-filled field to go skate at the church. We would skate the rails in numerous ways, having them going down a curb, or linking them together to create ultra-long rails. The tricks we learned included feeble grinds, smith grinds, k-grinds, salad grinds, and lipslides. Practicing the same rail tricks over and over again increased our confidence and prepared us for what was to come in the middle of March.

In the beginning of March, the overwhelmingly cold and skin freezing temperatures began to let up. As the middle of March neared, the days became warmer and warmer, and soon the snow began to melt. As more and more concrete began to show, we started visiting different skate spots to see which rail was going to be our first spring feat. We drove around town, scouting, and eventually found the perfect six stair rail: it was square, blue, and it promised frontside skating for my friends and I. Now, although we had boardslided a few rails the year before, the fact was none of us had actually grinded a rail. So that day we convinced ourselves we were going to do more than just boardslides, the rail was going to be grinded, too—eventually.

On Saturday we got ready and went and skated some ledges at City Hall. We began doing 50-50's and 5-0's. Feeling a little anxious we climbed into the van and drove to the 33rd Street rail we had found a few days earlier. The run-up was short but it was still possible. There were three of us who were ready for the rail, or so we thought. The other four guys just waited around watching and cheering us on. We began by doing some ollies down the stairs and the spectators told us whether we would have enough height to make it onto the rail if we tried. We began getting scared because the warm-up was over; we had all the practice we needed and now it was time to step it up and do it.

It didn't matter that he was laying on the ground. Chris had actually tried it.

We all began by approaching the stairs, busting an ollie, and sort of kicking our board out in mid-air towards the rail. "Okay, I am going to do it this try" must have been repeated a thousand times. Finally, Chris said, "Okay, this time, right here." But thinking that he was going to chicken out we did not hold our breaths. He approached the rail and popped an ollie. A fraction of a second later he landed on the rail and his board slipped out. He fell to the bottom of the stairs and rolled onto his side.

It didn't matter that he was laying on the ground. Chris had actually tried it.

"What was it like?" I yelled.

"It was easier than I thought; you just got to try it," he replied, his eyes gleaming with possibility.

So it was my turn. I rode up to the stairs and popped an ollie, throwing my board onto the rail. I landed in a grind position but then jumped off. Next, my other friend Terry tried it; he actually grinded to the bottom before he fell off. We had made the jump from dreaming about rails to actually trying them. Instantly, we understood what it meant: we had entered a new dimension of skateboarding. It was unbelievable and we began yelling due to our incredible excitement.

After what seemed like an hour of ollieing onto the rail and grinding it, we all successfully did it. The snapping sound of an ollie, the metallic grind of truck to rail, and the crisp landing of wheels sounded just like the skate videos we had seen. The experience was overwhelming and we were so excited because now we could actually say we had grinded a rail. It was huge! Now that we had one rail under our belts, we would be able to try others.

The following summer after our first rail experience, my friends and I made a trip out to Vancouver. We were filming for a skate video that we were going to make. The reason we chose Vancouver was because we knew that it was home to some of the nicest handrails in Canada. Our trip was spent mostly at the CIBC building in Vancouver, which featured a six-stair rail, an eight-stair rail, and even a ten-stair rail. Needless to say, our first session at the spot resulted in more than a 50-50 going down. The cool thing about the trip was that we did not get kicked out of the spots right away, giving us more time to build up our confidence. Skating with everyone created serious energy that we all seemed to feed off.

The great thing about skateboarding handrails is that it gets your adrenaline pumping, which increases your confidence to try other tricks. When we were skating the CIBC rail, we began warming up with boardslides, noseslides and 50-50's, but by the end of the day the tricks that had been done included a salad grind, front boardslides, smith grinds and feeble grinds. The salad grind was done by my friend Chris after he had attempted a bluntslide but accidently shifted himself into salad footing. Although he did not land it, he did realize it was easier than it looked, and he switched his attempts from bluntslide to salad grind and within about ten tries he was rolling away victorious.

Learning how to skate rails is a slow process, usually beginning with a little flat bar. It takes time to be able to work your way up to actually sliding down a real one. The good thing is that once you begin skating real rails you can progress quite rapidly. Often when I have gone to skate a rail I end up doing more than I expected. Usually if the fear does not get to you, and you actually begin trying to skate the rail, you start to get a feel for it and the adrenaline causes you to try other tricks.

The First Rail Skateboarders

Natas Kaupas

Natas Kaupas was one of the first skateboarders to think of riding handrails. He was a legend in his time and is still talked about today. He turned pro for Santa Monica Airlines in 1985 and was one of the first pro's to get a signature shoe. Natas got his own signature shoe through Etnies. We all know Etnies now, but back in the mid-80's Etnies was a relatively new and unknown company. At the time his shoe came out there were only three major skateboarding shoe companies within the industry. Those shoe companies were Airwalk, Vans and Vision Street Wear. Airwalk had Tony Hawk among its top riders, Vans had Steve Caballero, and Vision had Gator. All three of them were vert skateboarders. However, Etnies, when most companies chose to deal with the more popular vert riders, broke with tradition and took a risk in investing its signature shoe in a street skater.

For most pro's, the success of board sales and fame are closely related. People tend to buy boards based on the skateboarder's talent and the other part is based on the graphic of the boards. Natas had both aspects working in his favor. Everyone knew him for his talent, which was unmatched in his street style and innovation; and everyone was drawn to his awesome "black panther" board graphics, which came in various designs, such as the panther as a kitty or as a full-sized animal. The graphic became immensely popular and it only served to increase Natas' fame.

The name Natas was marked with much intrigue as individuals and speculation contributed to his rebel image. Kids speculated that his parents were devil worshippers and that they had chosen the name Natas because, when spelled backwards, it read "Satan". Many youths started rumors that he was a devil worshiper, which led to more attention being put on him both as a person and a skateboarder. The real story, however, is that Natas' Lithuanian parents had been expecting a girl and they had already picked out the names Natasha and Natalia. So, when a son was born, they decided to name him Natas, which was

The idea of trying a handrail had never been thought of before, much less attempted.

also used as a surname in Lithuania. Whatever the story was, controversy and rumors only helped to bring more attention to this amazing skateboarder.

Natas surpassed expectations when he went on to pioneer the way for a new style of skateboarding. One of the most famous tricks he invented was the Natas spin. The Natas spin was characterized by an ollie onto a fire hydrant, followed with a spin on the top and then a quick pop off. Natas was also one of the first skateboarders to try and ride a rail. During a contest in Del Mar in 1985, he tried a boardslide off the stage rail. The idea of trying a handrail had never been thought of before, much less attempted (with the possible exception being Mark Gonzales). Although he never landed the boardslide, his move sparked a revolution. Natas Kaupas, along with Mark Gonzales, would go on to be one of the first skateboarders to slide and grind a handrail.

Mark Gonzales

When one thinks of legendary skateboarders from the past, one inevitably thinks of Mark Gonzales. Mark Gonzales is not only a professional skateboarder but he is also a company owner, artist and poet. He does not only ride skateboards, but he sells them too, having started his own company, Krooked Skateboards, which is distributed through Deluxe in San Francisco. Over the years he has also built up a reputation as a talented artist, having done shows throughout the United States and Europe. Moreover, Mark has used his art in combination with skateboarding, often featuring his work on boards. And, always one to try new things, he has appeared in commercials for television and in a cult film called "Gummo."

His name is hailed among the top pros of today as being a leader and pioneer in street skateboarding. In reading over interviews with pro skateboarders, one will discover that Mark Gonzales is still mentioned as one of the top-five most influential figures in the sport. One of the reasons why Mark Gonzales enjoys such a reputation is because he, alongside pros like Natas, led the way in advancing street skating. In the early years of the sport he was often seen cruising the streets and popping ollies. It was not a trick he invented, but it was one he certainly took to new limits. In fact, some think that he was one of the first people to actually ollie onto a curb. And, if that is not enough, Mark Gonzales is also credited as one of the first people to successfully slide a handrail.

In the September 2006 issue of *Transworld Skateboarding*, Mark Gonzales was awarded The 2006 Legend Award. Mackenzie Eisenhour, in the same issue of *Transworld*, wrote that Rodney Mullen, with all his invented tricks, was one of two individuals who had profoundly transformed the sport of skateboarding; the other, he claimed, was Mark Gonzales. He went on to credit Mark Gonzales with the following tricks:

1984 – The first one to ollie up curbs

1985 – The first to do a kickflip on the street

1986 – The first to do frontside pop shove-its on street

1986 – The first to frontside boardslide an eight-stair rail and backside boardslide on another rail

1986 – The first to venture into the world of switch stance with a switch method at Savanah Slamma contest

1986 – The first person to ollie the huge gap at Embarcadero that was named "The Gonz" gap

1991 – The first to tuck-knee the Wallenberg four

1991 – The first to caveman darkslide a rail

1991 – The first to boardslide the huge double-kink rail at Santa Monica Elementary School

1991 – The first to noseslide the Wishire seven-stair rail

Mark Gonzales' first major sponsor was Vision Skateboards. After riding for Vision he went on to co-found a new skateboard company with World Industries owner, Steve Rocco. The two created Blind Skateboards, which is still around to this day. The name Blind was a jab at the concept of Vision, a deliberate mockery of his former sponsor. After several years with Blind, he parted ways with the company and joined forces with Real Skateboards. His connection to Real Skateboards has been longstanding, so much so that even with the advent of his new skateboard company, Krooked, he has maintained a close relationship with Real. In fact, the company that distributes Real also distributes for his new company.

In his formative years, Mark Gonzales led the way in gnarly handrail skating. One rail in particular, a rail that confirmed his god-like status, was a double-stair kinked rail that went from five stairs, to flat, to another five stairs. Although nowadays one can flip through any magazine and see someone skating a kinked rail, back then a double-set kinked rail was just not considered, let alone attempted. The scary thing was that the rail was round and it had a considerable drop on the one side. This trick was featured for his part in the Blind video called "Video Days." The part was revolutionary because Gonzales demonstrated insanely progressive tricks on rails, such as a frontside 180 to switch 50-50 on a six-stair rail. Since then, as the years have passed, not only has Mark Gonzales continued to skate rails, but his video parts often feature him skating street and ramps as well.

Proof of Mark Gonzales' immense influence is that he has stood the test of time. He began professional skateboarding in the early 80's and continues to ride professionally to this day. While fads have come and gone, he has kept skating, and to this day his video parts highlight the fun he still has when he is on his board, whether it be doing rails, skating ramps, or cruising around skating street.

Jamie Thomas King of Rails

One of the most influential and well-known skateboarders has got to be Jamie Thomas. He emerged on the skateboard scene in the late 90's. He came on the scene as a true skateboarder, someone who loved the sport and lived, ate, and breathed skateboarding. Jamie Thomas moved from Alabama to southern California in search of making it as a pro skateboarder. He had very little money and support in his move out to California and it is said that he actually was homeless for a short time after his move. His early sponsors included Real, Experience, Invisible and later Toy Machine.

His first real thrust into the limelight was a *Transworld* interview in which they followed Jamie around for a period of twenty-four hours. One of the opening pictures was of Jamie standing with his shirt off in front of a mirror, shaving his head with a razor. Across his lower back is tattooed the word "Independent." The interview followed him around and captured him doing insane tricks, tricks bigger and gnarlier than usual, many of them down rails or stairs.

Jamie Thomas also came out with two great video parts. The first one was "Heavy Metal" (1994), and the second most memorable was "Welcome To Hell" (1996). By the second video, Jamie Thomas had earned the right to have the last section of the video in the all-star cast of "Welcome to Hell," the part reserved for the best skateboarder on the team. His Toy Machine section was awesome as it combined street skating with large stairs and gaps earning him a place in skateboard folklore. In the opening to his part, he is seen skateboarding across a bridge matched perfectly to the opening of his song. As he skates across the screen, an Iron Maiden song slowly builds, bit by bit, into a fast-paced heavy metal anthem. As the music progresses, so does the skateboarding.

The opening tricks are a backside lipslide down a handrail, followed by a long backside 50-50 down another, even larger handrail. What is most impressive is that they are done in the same run, one after the other. From there the video part gets crazier and crazier, with larger rails, bigger drops, and a speed that seems impossible, not only for its time, but even today. As a matter of fact, it may be argued that this one video part sparked the whole rail craze that has existed in skateboarding since then.

After Jamie Thomas' epic part in the Toy Machine video, he went on to form his own company called Zero. The company started with riders who rode in a style similar to his own. The riders were mostly rail skaters; the team's first members included Jim Greco, Matt Mumford, Adrian Lopez and Jamie Thomas. The first video superseded expectations as the skaters skated every kind of rail in sight, the most memorable part being the fallen light post which they slid and grinded every which way. The Zero video not only led to a revolution in tricks, but it also transformed the filming of skate videos.

The Zero video used a new format of filming, which consisted mainly of wide-angle lenses and close-up shots—shots that gave special emphasis to the grinds and slides. The wide-angle lens provided viewers with a different perspective, as it showed just how big the rails and gaps truly were. The quick shots and rapid editing of scenes used in the video also added dramatic effect, putting the emphasis on speed and giving the video a fast-paced feel. This new technique in filming was quickly adapted by other skateboard companies and is still widely used today. It is a change largely attributable to Jamie Thomas.

Jamie Thomas was once interviewed in *Thrasher* magazine and asked what had been some of the scariest tricks he had done or attempted. It was a serious question, considering the fact that during his career he had grinded some huge rails, ollied some crazy gaps, and slid some crazy ledges. The two tricks that Thomas said were his scariest were the Leap of Faith, and a backside 5-0 down a twenty-stair rail that he did in "Welcome to Hell."

The Leap of Faith was a two-story drop over a rail onto flat concrete. When trying the almost suicidal gap, he broke his board from the impact. Luckily, he walked away unscathed. In reality, it did not matter that Thomas failed to roll out; what was amazing was that he had attempted it in the first place. Others were not so fortunate. When another boy tried it later, he broke both his legs from the fall. Again, it only goes to show how truly talented Jamie Thomas is.

Zero Skateboards has been one of the most popular board companies in the past six years and it is due in large part to Jamie

It may be argued that this one video part sparked the whole rail craze that has existed in skateboarding since then.

Thomas. He has continued to come out with awesome video parts and has formed a team of insane, fearless rail skaters. He has taken rail skating to a whole new level and, in the years ahead, it looks like he will only continue to be an innovative force in the sport.

www.thrashermagazine.com

Mark Appleyard

Mark Appleyard was born in Ontario, Canada in 1982. He began skateboarding when he was eleven years old. He grew up skating the park near his home, as well as the urban streets of Toronto. Mark Appleyard began gaining national coverage within Canada through the video magazine *Skate Canada* and the magazine *Concrete Powder*. Eventually, this coverage led to him being recognized by major companies in the United States and he ended up getting sponsored by Alien Workshop. However, the relationship soon ended and he made the switch to Flip Skateboards, the company he continues to ride for to this day.

Prior to Mark Appleyard's appearance on the skate scene, most skateboarders were grinding and sliding handrails with only basic tricks, such as 5-0's, 50-50's, Smith grinds and Feeble grinds. But Appleyard raised the bar when he was featured in skateboard magazines doing nollie heelflip noseslides down rails. People could not believe what they were seeing, a technical flip trick being applied to a large rail. It was a trick that combined the fear factor with technical ability. Pictures also caught him nollie flip backside 50-50'ing down a large hubba, as well as nollie flip k-grinding the Beverly Hills High School rail. Rightly enough, Mark Appleyard's amazing style and technical tricks led him to win the coveted Skater of the Year award in 2003, given out by *Thrasher* magazine.

Although Mark Appleyard was one of the first skaters to really bring technical flip tricks to rails, there are those who have been expanding on this way of skating and have taken it to new levels. The skateboarders who have been at the forefront of this new type of rail skating have included John Allie, Billy Marks, and Heath Kirchart. The technical tricks they have regularly done include kickflips to boardslides, grinds, tailslides, noseslides and lipslides.

John Allie came onto the scene with his epic part in the Zero video "Dying to Live," in which he flipped into almost every one of his rail tricks, the most impressive ones being a kickflip frontside tailslide and a kickflip frontside lipslide. Then there is Heath Kirchart, a veteran skater who has continued to progress and lead the way over the years. He is one of the first people to have performed kickflip frontside boardslides down a rail, and he has gone on to do kickflip frontside 50-50's, and kickflip backside lipslides and tailslides.

Finally, there is Billy Marks, a rider who skates for Toy Machine skateboards, a rider often considered to be a master of flip tricks onto rails and ledges. His tricks include kickflips to boardslides, both frontside and backside, as well as kickflip frontside 50-50's and kickflip lipslides. Although there are certainly other skaters who produce compelling flip tricks to grinds, it's Allie, Kirchart and Marks who are currently at the front of the pack.

Geoff Rowley

Geoff Rowley was born in Liverpool, England in 1976, and began skating at a young age. When looking at Geoff Rowley's small frame and weak little mustache, one would never expect to find a rail destroyer underneath it all. Geoff Rowley has got to be one of the best skateboarders to watch; his video parts are intense and aggressive and he is said to be one of the hardest working skaters in the industry. From video to video his parts are chock-full of huge gaps, giant ledges and rails. His accomplishments, which are vast, include winning the *Thrasher* magazine Skater of the Year award in 2000, a most prestigious award because it is only given to one professional skateboarder per year.

Geoff Rowley skated for Flip before his move to America. He then moved to America when he was eighteen to further pursue his career. Flip skateboards began in England, but under a different name. It was formerly known as Deathbox skateboards and began in the early 1990's. The two co-founders were Ian Deacon and Jeremy Fox. Jeremy and Ian eventually left England with the hopes of making Deathbox a legitimate, well-known skateboard company in America. Wanting a catchier name to build upon, a name with more brand power, they decided to change the company name from Deathbox to Flip. Some of their early riders included Geoff Rowley, Rune Glifberg and Tom Penny. What is most remarkable, especially in a sport where team loyalty changes so often, is that all three continue to ride for Flip and have had spectacular skateboarding careers.

When Geoff Rowley was interviewed by Ed Templeton in 2000, he was asked what motivated him to attempt big rails and ledges. His answer: personal problems that resulted from his girlfriend breaking up

> **He said that the pain pushed him and he used skateboarding as a way to escape.**

with him. He said that the pain pushed him and he used skate-boarding as a way to escape. He also claimed the hardships from his failed relationship helped him because he did not care if he got hurt. Whatever Rowley's motivation for doing large rails, he defi-nitely has confidence in his ability, and he mixes it with an almost unmatched fearlessness.

www.skateboarding.com

Geoff Rowley's fame began to increase when he was featured in ads for Vans Shoes, skating a massive hubba ledge in front of the Staples Center in Los Angeles. The advertisement—now famous—featured him doing a noseslide, as well as a 50-50. Just how big is the ledge in question? Well, after moving to Los An-geles I ended up skating by this ledge and learned first hand how large it truly was; pictures did not do it justice. The ledge at the top of the stairs was as high as my shoulder, and I am around 5'10". There are eighteen stairs in total and to get onto the ledge, because it is so high, one has to fully commit and launch way out. To skate it requires laser-like precision and downright fearless-ness. The ledge just goes to show that Geoff Rowley is not the average skateboarder.

When asked about skating big ledges and rails in an interview, he was quoted saying, "I don't just jump on big ledges and handrails every day; I like to skate all kinds of little stupid things–curbs and whatnot. But I get full release on the big stuff" (Rowley, 2000). Many of Geoff Rowley's insane rails have been done in Vans shoes; some like the old-school low-cut Vans that provide little to no support for huge impacts. Perhaps the thin soles help provide motivation for Geoff not to bail on his tricks. Whatever the case, with the way he has continued to ride over the years, he should not change a thing.

www.skateboarding.com/skate

Skateboarding is Changing

Perhaps rail skaters are partially crazy because they risk their bodies in an attempt to achieve an adrenaline rush and because they always try tricks that are bigger and more dangerous than before. They are always pushing the boundaries and limits of what can be done. These individuals possess the ability to shut down the part of the brain that warns them of imminent danger. Instead of second-guessing themselves, they trust wholeheartedly in their ability to do a trick. For many of them it is a combination of feeling and logic. Although these individuals take serious risks, the risks they take are not blind and reckless. Their logic tells them what can be done; and their feeling tells them it has to be done—or at least tried.

Rail skateboarding is truly all about calculated risk. The individuals who excel at doing rails do so because they are precise in the tricks they do. They do not just flail themselves at a rail and hope they land it. Each attempt is done with split-second maneuvering, all of which is coded within their muscle memory, a memory built upon years of practice. Their brains know exactly what to do. In mid-air, if a skater realizes the trick cannot be landed, his or her brain will react within a split-second and move into recovery mode. The trick is forgotten and the thought becomes how best to bail out. Because the skater has bailed out doing the same trick on smaller stuff in the past, his or her muscle memory knows exactly how to kick out the board, how to lean, and where flailing feet need to go. Muscle memory provides these answers in a fraction of a second. It is the difference between walking away from a massive rail and going to the hospital with a broken leg.

Today skateboarding seems to be progressing at a faster speed than ever before. About four years ago, a friend of mine moved to a bigger city that was known for its progressive skateboard scene. The city was full of sick street spots, rails, and skate parks. He could not get over how much better the kids in that city were compared to ours. Hearing him tell me how good the young kids were made me consider why some cities have better skateboarders. Was it something in the water that made individuals better in certain cities?

I soon learned that it was not in the water; in large part it had to do with something called synergy. Nowadays many skaters advance quickly in the sport because skate parks are more common than ever before; they act like focal points, drawing in a critical mass of skate talent from around the city. This is key because it gives

Skateboarding, right from its earliest days, has been about pure enjoyment and having a creative outlet.

up-and-coming skaters not only an ideal environment to practice tricks, but also a place where they can learn by watching and studying others. Skaters build off the energy at these parks; they push and challenge each other, and the friendly competition only fosters greater and greater skill. The last five years are evidence of this trend. Cities are producing larger numbers of quality amateur skateboarders and, as they feed off each other's energy, progression within the sport has only increased.

Greater progression has also fuelled fiercer competition. With the advent of high-paying sponsorships, personal clothing lines and video game royalties, aspiring skaters are being forced to step it up a notch every time they go out and skate. This has resulted in a ten-fold increase in talent. And because the stakes are so high, this increase is taking place over a shorter period of time. Growing up, many kids took years before they landed their first kickflip; today it seems normal for kids to learn them within a month or two.

Besides the prevalence of new skateparks, another thing that has helped spark this synergy is the amount of videos and magazines that young kids are watching. Skateboarding companies are continuously competing to come out with the best new video. Due to the over-saturation of the market, with insane skateboard videos coming out by the day, kids everywhere are thinking it is normal to grind twelve-stair rails and jump down large gaps, whereas in the past it was thought to be only possible for the elite pros.

This movement towards crazier tricks has brought with it an inevitable result: injuries. The horror stories are endless, but one will suffice. After his move to the big city, my friend told me about the insane little rail mongers he had met since arriving. One kid, who was about thirteen years old, was jumping off stairs and down rails like he had wings. He had an intense desire to get sponsored and figured the fastest way towards this goal was by trying massive gaps and rails. My friend later informed me that within two years the kid had to quit skating because he had damaged the growth plates in his shins. The continuous pounding on the ground from jumping off of things had supposedly damaged the bones in his shin so badly that doctors thought the bones might never grow to their natural size. If that was not enough, the kid was also reportedly having serious knee problems as well.

The point of the story is that instead of trying to be the next Jamie Thomas, this kid should have been learning what makes skateboarding so much fun. He had forgotten one of skateboardings primary beliefs: the belief that fun and creativity come before the nasty world of competition, coaches and fame. First and foremost, skateboarders ought to explore new ways of skating the environment around them. The basic motivation should never be intense training just for the prize of temporary recognition. The whole point of skateboarding, and the reason it has attracted its specific crowd, is because it is about hanging out with friends, skating around and learning new tricks. It is for the rush, the feeling, and the love of the sport; not because one wants to get sponsored.

One of the challenges that comes with skateboarding's increasing notoriety is that it is attracting a whole new crowd compared to years gone by. The reality, and a fear held by all true skaters, is that with more people joining the sport it could eventually become like the rest of the sports world—a world which focuses on fierce competition, money and heroes. In reality, many veteran skaters believe the focus of the sport has already begun to make the shift, from having fun with friends and skating for the sheer fun of it, to trying to be the absolute best and to gain recognition. While it is certainly good to have goals, skaters—both new and old alike—should remember that skateboarding, right from its earliest days, has been about pure enjoyment and having a creative outlet.

The aggressive, rail-ripping, gap-destroying Geoff Rowley summed it up best in one of his interviews. The interviewer asked him about his favorite spot to visit and Rowley told him it was Liverpool, England, because it reminded him of the innocent times he had when he grew up skateboarding. He talked about how on Saturdays and Sundays as he was growing up, he and his friends would get up at 8:30 a.m. to catch a bus into the city so they could go skate all day, and how, when they came back, they would continue skating around his house all night. To me, that is the way skateboarding should be. It is about hanging out with friends, pushing oneself to the limits, and not letting skateboarding become like another jock sport, full of cocky macho dirt bags that are into cars and bomber jackets.

Trick Tips

Caveman Boardslide

1 Stand at the top of the stairs holding your board with your left hand if you are regular footed, or right hand if you are goofy footed.

2 Run up to the rail to get momentum for your jump.

3 Jump at the rail holding the board in front of you.

4   Aim for the middle of the board to land on the rail.

5   Before your board hits the rail, jump on your board with both feet landing over the bolts.

6   Moments after your feet land on the board you will then land on the rail.

7 Keep your knees bent and lean forward to keep your balance as you slide.

8 When you are nearing the end of the rail, turn your shoulders back so that your front shoulder is facing forward.

9 As your shoulders turn, bring the rest of your body around as well.

The secret to this trick is to lean forward as you land on the rail.

10 When you land, bend your knees for absorption.

Backside Boardslide

1 Ride up with your back facing the rail.

2 As you near the edge of the stairs, pop an ollie.

3 When you ollie, turn your board 90 degrees.

4 Aim your ollie so that you land with the rail in the middle of the board.

5 Balance your weight over the front and back trucks.

6 Lean forward as you get on the rail to keep from slipping out.

7 When you near the end of the rail, turn your shoulders back 90 degrees and turn your feet as well.

8 When you land, bend your knees for absorption.

The secret to this trick is to make sure you land with your body and board completely intersecting the rail.

Frontside Boardslide

1   Ride up with your front facing the rail.

2   When you near the edge of the stairs, pop an ollie.

3   Ollie and turn your board 90 degrees, but keep your shoulders parallel with the rail.

4   Keep your eyes focused on the rail and where you will be landing in order to maintain balance.

5   Land with the center of your board on the rail. Your board can land flat on the rail or angled up slightly.

6 Keep your balance by placing your weight evenly on the front trucks and your tail.

7 When you near the end of the rail, turn your board and lower body back 90 degrees.

8 When you land, bend your knees for absorption.

The secret to this trick is to keep your shoulders and head facing forward to stop you from slipping out.

Backside Bigspin Boardslide to Fakie

1 Ride up with your front facing the rail.

2 Place your front foot four inches below the bottom bolts on your front truck.

3 Place your back foot in the ollie position.

4   Ollie a foot away from the rail.

5   Ride up to the rail at a 30 degree angle.

6   Pop a backside pop shovit near the edge of the stairs.

7   As the board finishes spinning the 180 shovit, extend your legs slightly so that the board is now fully contacting your feet.

8 As the board hits your feet, turn the remaining 30 degrees so that you land in boardslide position.

9 When the middle of the board is over the rail in the air, extend your legs slightly so that you land on the rail in a controlled manner. Be sure that your shoulders are facing forward to keep from slipping out.

The secret to this trick is popping a nice shovit so that you are in control when you land on the rail.

10 When you reach the end of the rail, turn your body so that you land riding backwards.

11 When you land, bend your knees for absorption.

Frontside 50-50 Grind

1 Approach the rail riding parallel with no more than a foot between you and the rail. Your front should be facing the rail.

2 Place your front foot slightly below the bottom bolts on your front truck with your back foot in the ollie position.

3 Pop an ollie near the edge of the stairs.

4 Aim your ollie so that you land with the rail in the middle of both trucks.

5 Since the rail is slanted down, you will need to extend your front foot down slightly so that both your trucks land on the rail at the same time.

6 Lean into the rail with your leading shoulder in order to keep your balance.

The secret to this trick is to have your 50-50's on flat bars consistent, that way you can maintain your balance when you get on the rail. The rail must land in the middle of the trucks.

7   As you grind off the end of the rail, lift up slightly by applying pressure to your tail.

8   When you land, bend your knees for absorption.

Backside 50-50 Grind

1 Approach the rail riding parallel or at a slight angle, with no more than a foot between you and the rail. Your back should be facing the rail.

2 Place your front foot slightly below the bottom bolts on your front truck.

3   Place your back foot in the ollie position.

4   Pop an ollie near the edge of the stairs.

5   Aim your ollie so that you land with the rail in the middle of
      both trucks.

6 Since the rail is slanted down, you will need to extend your front leg slightly so that both trucks land in the middle of the rail at the same time.

7 Lean into the rail with your leading shoulder so that you keep your balance.

The secret to this trick is in popping a well-controlled ollie so that you get into the grind with both trucks landing on the middle of the rail.

8   As you grind, keep your knees bent.

9   As you grind off the end of the rail, lift up your front truck slightly by applying pressure to your tail.

10 When you land, bend your knees for absorption.

Frontside 5-0 Grind

1 Approach the rail riding parallel, with no more than a foot between you and the rail. Your front should be facing the rail.

2 Place your front foot slightly below the bottom bolts on your front truck. Your back foot should be in the ollie position.

3 Pop an ollie near the edge of the stairs.

4 Aim your ollie as if you were going to do a 50-50.

5 Instead of letting your front foot come down on the rail as you would a 50-50, push down with your back foot so that you land in 5-0.

6 When you land in grind tilt your shoulders forward slightly so that you do not slip backwards.

7 As you grind off the rail transfer your weight to the center of the board and bend your knees for impact.

The secret to this trick is to ollie straight out from the stairs as you would an ollie. Since the rail slopes down your straight ollie will put you in the 5-0 position.

Backside 5-0 Grind

1 Approach the rail riding parallel, with no more than a foot between you and the rail. Your back should be facing the rail.

2 Place your front foot slightly below the bottom bolts on your front truck. Your back foot should be in the ollie position.

3   Pop an ollie near the edge of the stairs.

4   Aim your ollie as if you were going to do a backside 50-50.

5   Instead of letting your front foot come down on the rail as you
    would a 50-50, push down with your back foot so that you
    land in 5-0.

6 When you begin grinding tilt your shoulders slightly forward so that you do not slip backwards.

7 When you land, bend your knees for absorption.

The secret to this trick is to ollie straight out from the stairs as you would an ollie. Since the rail slopes down your straight ollie will put you in the 5-0 position.

Backside Feeble Grind

1 Ride up with your back facing the rail.

2 Come in at a 30 degree angle.

3 Place your front foot five inches below the bottom bolts on your front truck.

4   Place your back foot in the ollie position.

5   Pop an ollie near the edge of the stairs.

6   Your ollie should be a mixture of a boardslide and a backside 50-50.

7   Ollie so that your back truck lands on the rail. To hold the
    grind position, your truck should land with your outside wheel
    firmly pressed against the rail.

8   Keep your weight over your back leg with your front foot
    simply resting and guiding your board. Tilt the nose of your

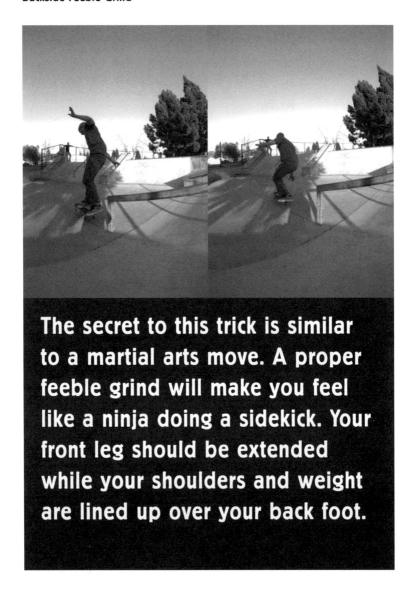

The secret to this trick is similar to a martial arts move. A proper feeble grind will make you feel like a ninja doing a sidekick. Your front leg should be extended while your shoulders and weight are lined up over your back foot.

board downwards to hold the feeble position.

9 As you grind off the rail, press down on your tail to level your board out as you prepare to hit the ground and bring your front foot and board around so that you land straight.

10 When you land, bend your knees for absorption.

Frontside Feeble Grind

1   Ride up with your front facing the rail.

2   Come in at a 30 degree angle.

3   Place your front foot four inches below the bottom bolts on your front truck. Angle your front foot upwards slightly.

4 Place your back foot in the ollie position.

5 When you near the edge of the stairs, pop an ollie.

6 Your ollie will be a mixture of a frontside boardslide and a frontside 50-50.

7 Ollie straight onto your back truck, landing with your outside back wheel being firmly pressed against the rail.

8 All of your weight should be over your back leg. Your front foot should simply be resting and guiding your board. Tilt the nose of your board downwards to hold the feeble position.

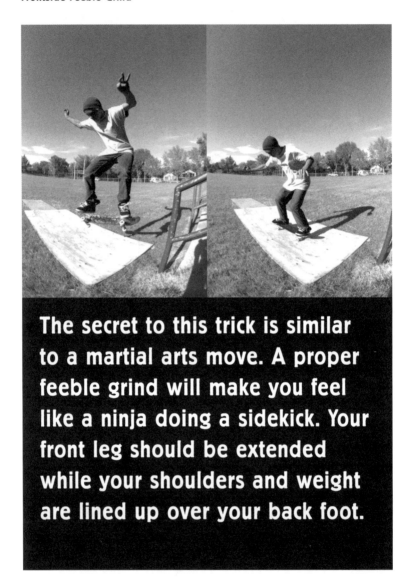

The secret to this trick is similar to a martial arts move. A proper feeble grind will make you feel like a ninja doing a sidekick. Your front leg should be extended while your shoulders and weight are lined up over your back foot.

9 As you grind off the rail, press down on your tail to level your board out as you prepare to hit the ground, and turn your board and body slightly to land straight.

10 When you land, bend your knees for absorption.

Frontside Salad Grind

1 Ride up with your front facing the rail.

2 Approach the rail at a 30 degree angle.

3 Place your front foot five inches from the bottom bolts on your front truck.

4 Angle your front foot upwards slightly on the board.

5 Your back foot should be in the ollie position.

6 Pop an ollie near the edge of the stairs.

7 Try and land in a crooked 5-0 grind. Think of it as being a cross between a 5-0 and a bluntslide.

8   As you land in the salad grind position, keep your shoulders facing forward and your eyes looking forward as well.

9   Your tail should be pressed against the rail, which will help hold you in the grind position.

The secret to this trick is to turn from your waist downwards into a crooked 5-0 grind while your upper body remains parallel with the rail. Also, your outside back wheel should be pressed firmly into the rail.

10 As you near the end of the grind, turn your feet slightly so that you land straight.

11 When you land, bend your knees for absorption.

Backside Salad Grind

1 Ride up with your back facing the rail.

2 Approach the rail at a 30 degree angle.

3 Your front foot should be six inches from the bottom bolts on your front truck.

4   Your front foot should be angled slightly upwards.

5   Your back foot should be in the ollie position.

6   Pop an ollie near the edge of the stairs.

7   Land in a crooked 5-0 grind. Think of it as being in between
    a backside 5-0 and a bluntslide.

8 As you near the end of the grind, turn your board slightly so that you land straight.

9 When you land, bend your knees for absorption.

The secret to this trick is to land with your tail pressed firmly into the rail to ensure you keep your balance.

Backside Salad Grind Frontside 180 Out

1 Ride up with your back facing the rail.

2 Approach the rail at a 30 degree angle.

3 Your front foot should be six inches from the bottom bolts on
   your front truck.

4 Angle your front foot upwards slightly on the board.

5 Place your back foot in the ollie position.

6 Pop an ollie near the edge of the stairs.

7 Land in a crooked 5-0 grind. Think of it as being in between a backside 5-0 and a bluntslide.

8 Land with your back truck being crooked on the rail and your tail pressed firmly into the rail. You should then begin grinding.

9 As you near the end of the grind, begin turning your shoulders 180 degrees.

The secret to this trick is to think of it as a mix between a 5-0 grind and a bluntslide. Also, when coming out begin to turn your shoulders before you reach the end of the rail.

10 As you swing your shoulders around, turn the rest of your body so that you turn around to fakie as you grind off the end of the rail.

11 When you land, bend your knees for absorption.

Frontside Noseslide

1   Ride up with your front facing the rail.

2   Approach the rail at a slight angle.

3   Have your front foot slightly below the bottom bolts on your front truck.

4 Your back foot should be in the ollie position.

5 Pop an ollie at the edge of the stairs and turn your shoulders as if you were doing a backside 180.

6 Stop the rotation of your shoulders at 90 degrees.

7   As your nose nears the rail, push your front wheels against the rail while also pushing down on your nose.

8   While you are in the air, keep your head facing the bottom of the stairs with your eyes on the landing.

The secret to this trick is to do a backside 90 degree turn and push your legs out so that you lock firmly into the noseslide position.

9 As you approach the end of the rail, begin to rotate your body and board back 90 degrees so that you can land.

11 When you land, bend your knees for absorption.

Backside Noseslide

1 Ride up with your back facing the rail.

2 Approach the rail at a slight angle.

3 Place your front foot slightly below the bottom bolts on your front truck.

4 Your back foot should be in the ollie position.

5 When you near the edge of the stairs, pop a frontside 180. Turn your shoulders as you ollie.

6 Stop the rotation of your shoulders at 90 degrees.

7   As your nose nears the rail, push your front wheels against the rail and apply pressure into the rail to hold the noseslide position.

8   When you approach the end of the rail, rotate your body and board back 90 degrees so that you can land.

9   When you land, bend your knees for absorption.

The secret to this trick is doing a solid 90 degree ollie and landing with your wheels pressed firmly into the rail, with pressure on the nose as well.

Frontside Tailslide

1 Ride up with your front facing the rail.

2 Approach the rail at a 30 degree angle.

3 Ollie a foot and a half away from the rail.

Frontside Taiilslide

4   Place your front foot about four inches from the bottom bolts on your front truck.

5   Place your back foot in the ollie position.

6   When you near the edge of the stairs, pop an ollie. Pop your ollie, turn your shoulders and body 90 degrees.

7 When you turn 90 degrees, you want to aim for your wheels to land into the side of the rail while your tail lands on top of the rail.

8 When you feel your tail is over the rail, push down and push your back wheels firmly into the rail. By firmly pressing your wheels into the rail, you are able to control your speed.

The secret to this trick is to pop a nice 90 degree ollie, landing with your body intersecting the rail and making a perfect T shape.

9   As you near the end of the rail, turn your shoulders back to regular, bringing the rest of your body with it.

10 When you land, bend your knees for absorption.

Backside Tailslide

1 Ride up with your back facing the rail.

2 Place your front foot about four inches from the bottom bolts on your front truck.

3 Approach the rail at a 30 degree angle. The angle will keep

you from sliding too fast.

4   Pop an ollie a foot and a half away from the rail.

5   Pop your ollie and turn your waist and lower body 90 degrees.
    Keep your shoulders and head facing forward. This will help
    ensure you do not slip out.

6   As you turn 90 degrees, land with your wheels hitting into the side of the rail while your tail lands on top of the rail.

7   When you feel your tail is over the rail, press down and press the wheels into the rail.

8   When you get into tailslide, be sure to keep your wheels firmly

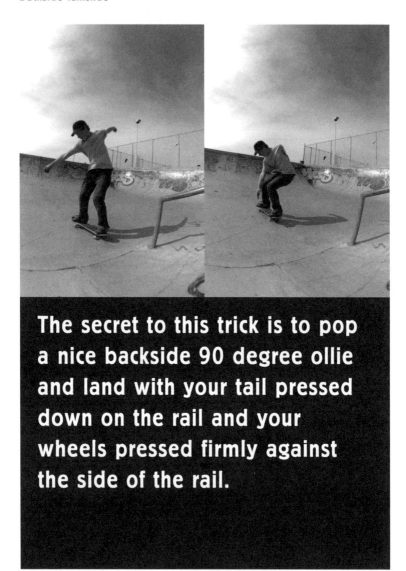

The secret to this trick is to pop a nice backside 90 degree ollie and land with your tail pressed down on the rail and your wheels pressed firmly against the side of the rail.

pressed against the rail, this helps control your speed. Be sure to keep your weight firmly on your tail as well.

9   As you near the end of the rail, turn your waist back to regular, bringing your legs and board with it.

10   Turn out and bend your knees for impact.

Frontside Lipslide

1 Ride up with your front facing the rail.

2 Approach the rail at a 30 degree angle.

3 Place your front foot about four inches from the bottom bolts on your front truck.

4 Your back foot should be in the ollie position.

5 When you near the edge of the stairs, pop a frontside 180.
   Pop your ollie and turn your shoulders and body.

6 Ollie out and over so that you are above the rail at a 90 degree angle.

7 Make sure the middle of the board lands on the rail.

8   When you are nearing contact with the rail, lean forward and have your weight evenly distributed over both trucks.

9   When you land on the rail, have your front foot over the bolts on your front truck and your back foot should be flat across the tail.

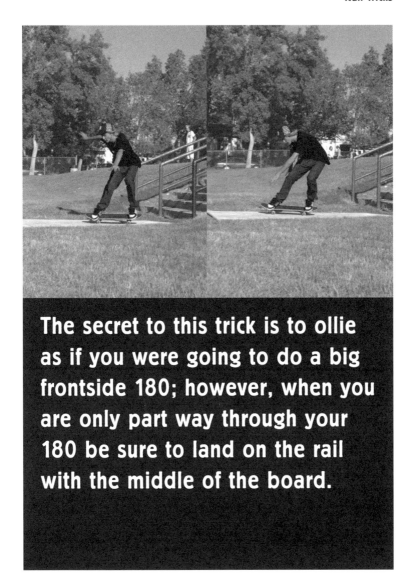

The secret to this trick is to ollie as if you were going to do a big frontside 180; however, when you are only part way through your 180 be sure to land on the rail with the middle of the board.

10 When you are nearing the end of your slide, turn your shoulders back 90 degrees and bring your lower body along with it.

11 When you land, bend your knees for absorption.

Backside Lipslide

1 Ride up with your back facing the rail.

2 Approach the rail at a 30 degree angle.

3 Place your front foot about four to six inches from the bottom bolts on your front truck.

4 Your back foot should be in the ollie position.

5 When you near the edge of the stairs, pop an ollie. Pop your ollie and turn your waist and lower body 90 degrees.

6 Keep your head and shoulders parallel with the rail and facing toward your landing. This enables you to keep your balance.

7   Ollie out and over so that you are above the rail at a 90 degree angle.

8   When you ollie out and over make sure the middle of the board lands on the rail.

9   When you are nearing the rail do not lean forward but keep your weight evenly centered over both trucks.

The secret to this trick is keeping your upper body parallel with the rail, while only your lower body does the 90 degree turn.

10 Land on the rail with your front foot over the bolts on your front truck and your back foot flat across the tail.

11 When you are nearing the end of your slide, turn your lower body back 90 degrees.

12 When you land, bend your knees for absorption.

Frontside Bluntslide To Fakie

1 Ride up with your front facing the rail.

2 Place your front foot four inches below the bottom bolts on your front truck.

3 Your back foot should be in the ollie position.

4   You want to be about a foot away from the rail when you ollie into the blunt position.

5   Approach the rail at a 30 degree angle.

6   When you near the edge of the stairs, pop your ollie.

7   Ollie into the rail so your back wheels just barely clear the rail

and slam your tail flat against it.

8   When you ollie, do not level out your board but keep it on an inclined angle.

9   Apply serious pressure to the tail so that it keeps your board propped up in the blunt position.

The secret to this trick is to apply pressure on your tail to hold the bluntslide. Also, when it comes time to slide out, just turn your shoulders toward the rail and your body and board will naturally begin turning with you.

10 Once you get into the blunt position, keep your shoulders turned slightly towards the landing to ensure you do not slip out.

11 As you reach the end of the rail, turn your shoulders around so that you are facing the rail and bring your lower body along with it.

12 When you land, bend your knees for absorption.

Backside Bluntslide

1   Ride up with your back facing the rail.

2   Your front foot should be four inches below the bottom bolts on your front truck.

3   Your back foot should be in the ollie position.

4   Approach the rail at a 35 degree angle.

5   When you near the edge of the stairs, pop your ollie.

6   Ollie into your blunt about a foot away from the rail.

7   Ollie into the rail so your back wheels just barely clear the rail and slam your tail flat against it.

8 When you ollie, do not level out your board but keep it on an inclined angle.

9 Apply serious pressure to the tail so that it keeps your board propped up in blunt position.

The secret to this trick is to approach at an angle and land with your tail firmly pressed against the rail.

10 When you get into the blunt position, your body should be facing forward as you slide along the rail.

11 As you reach the end of the rail, turn your shoulders and body 90 degrees so that you land riding forward.

12 When you land, bend your knees for absorption.

Frontside Nosebluntslide

1   Ride up with your front facing the rail.

2   Your front foot should be four inches below the bottom bolts on your front truck.

3   Your back foot should be in the ollie position.

4 Ollie a foot away from the rail.

5 Approach the rail at a 30 degree angle.

6 When you near the edge of the stairs, pop your ollie.

7 As you ollie, swing the board around as you would a 180, but in a manner that is more extreme. Incline your board upwards

on the ollie; and as you 180 extend your front foot down so the nose goes down, while you are also sucking your back foot up so the tail comes up.

8 Instead of doing the complete 180, only turn 90 degrees; aim your nose to land on the rail in noseblunt position.

The secret to this trick is in your ability to bring your nose down and your tail up as you 180.

9   As you land in noseblunt position, keep your weight over your front foot. Face your body forward as you slide down the rail.

10 When you near the end of the rail, turn your waist and feet back around 90 degrees so you are riding forward.

11 When you land, bend your knees for absorption.

Over Krooks

1 Ride up with your front facing the rail.

2 Approach the rail at a 20 degree angle.

3 Ollie a foot to a foot and a half away from the rail.

4   Place your front foot straight across the board, approximately two to three inches below the bottom bolts on your front truck. Place your back foot in the ollie position.

5   Ollie off the stairs and swing your shoulders around so they are at a 40 degree angle with your front shoulder leaning down into the rail.

6   Your front truck should land on the rail. The front wheel that was closest to the rail when you were riding up should be pressed into the rail to control your grind.

7   You want to consider the over krooks a combination of a noseblunt slide and a nosegrind.

The secret to this trick is to do an ollie as if you were going to nosegrind the rail, but push your back foot out away from the rail so you land in the over krooks position.

8 As you near the end of your grind, you want to bring your back foot and shoulders around slowly as you come off so that you land straight.

9 As you come out of the grind, bend your knees to absorb the impact of your landing.

Backside Nosegrind

1 Ride up with your back facing the rail.

2 Be a foot away from the rail when you begin your ollie.

3 Ride up almost parallel to the rail.

4   Place your front foot two inches below the bottom bolts on your front truck.

5   As you ollie, your legs will be bent in the air. When you get over the rail, extend your front leg so that your front truck lands in nosegrind. Keep your back leg bent so that your back truck stays in the air.

6 When you land in nosegrind, keep your weight on your front
   leg to hold the nosegrind position.

7 When you land in nosegrind it is important to land with the
   middle of your truck on the rail to ensure you do not slip out.

The secret to this trick is to land exactly with your front truck in the middle of the rail. It is also important you have enough speed because it will help you keep your balance.

8   As you near the end of your grind, give a little push off the end so your back truck clears the rail.

9   As you grind off the rail, extend your back leg and bend your front leg so that you level off for your landing.

10   When you land, bend your knees for absorption.

Frontside Smith Grind

1 Ride up with your front facing the rail.

2 Approach the rail at approximately a 20 degree angle.

3 Pop your ollie about a foot away from the rail.

4   Place your front foot four inches below the bottom bolts on your front truck. Place your back foot in the ollie position.

5   When you ollie, aim to land with your back truck on the rail.

6   Turn your board in the air so that your front wheels remain on the one side of the rail while your back truck lands on the rail.

7 Keep your weight on your back leg, holding your board in the grind position. This is best done by landing with your back foot on the tail as you make contact with the rail.

8 Press the board down lightly with your front foot as you grind.

The secret to this trick is landing with your weight over your back foot so you can actually grind. If you are having trouble grinding or you are falling forward, it means that you are not landing with all your weight on your back leg.

9   When you reach the end of the grind, lean back on your tail in order to bring up the nose of the board when you come out.

10 When you grind off the rail, suck your front foot up into your body so that your board levels off.

11 When you land, bend your knees for absorption.

Backside Smith Grind

1   Ride up with your back facing the rail.

2   Approach the rail at a 20 degree angle.

3   Pop your ollie a foot or a foot and a half away from the rail.

4   Place your front foot four inches below the bottom bolts on your front truck. Your back foot should be in the ollie position.

5   Pop your ollie and aim to land with your back truck on the rail.

6   Turn your board in the air so that your front wheels remain on the one side of the rail while your back truck lands on the rail.

Backside Smith Grind

7 Your back truck should land crooked on the rail with your outside wheel slammed tightly into the rail to hold your grind.

8 Keep your weight on your back leg, holding your board in the grind position.

9 Lightly press the front of your board downwards with your

The secret to backside smith grinds is landing with all of your weight over your back leg. It is important that your back outside wheel is pushed right against the side of the rail.

front foot as you grind.

10 When you reach the end of the grind, lean back on your tail right before you come out in order to bring up the nose of the board.

11 Grind off the rail and suck your front foot up into your body so that your board levels off and bend your knees for absorption.

K-Grind

1 Ride up with your back facing the rail.

2 Approach the rail at a 20 degree angle.

3 The toes on your front foot should be angled slightly upwards on your board. Place your front foot three inches from the

bottom bolts on your front truck.

4   Put your back foot in the ollie position.

5   Ollie about a foot to a foot and a half away from the rail.

6   Ollie and slide your front foot up so that your front foot lands on the nose.

7   As you ollie, have your truck land on the rail in a 35 degree angle. Your outside wheel should be pressed up against the rail to ensure your board stays in grind.

8   Keep your weight over your front foot; press your front foot down on the nose of your board as you make contact with the rail.

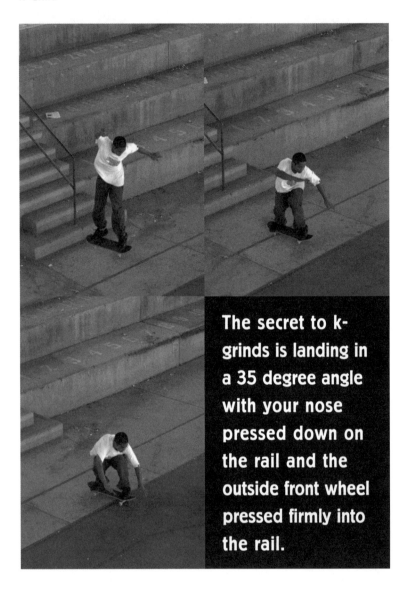

The secret to k-grinds is landing in a 35 degree angle with your nose pressed down on the rail and the outside front wheel pressed firmly into the rail.

9 As you grind the rail, extend your front leg while your back foot is bent holding you in the k-grind position.

10 As you come off the end of the rail, turn your front foot around slightly and your back foot around so you are straight when you ride away.

11 When you land, bend your knees for absorption.

Frontside Krooked Grind

1   Ride up with your front facing the rail.

2   Approach the rail at a 20 degree angle.

3   Angle your front foot slightly upwards. Place your front foot
    two inches from the bottom bolts on your front truck.

4   Place your back foot in the ollie position.

5   When you ride up to the edge of the stairs, ollie about a foot away from the rail.

6   When you ollie and are about to land on the rail, turn your back foot out and extend your front leg.

7 When you make contact with the rail, push down on your nose to hold the grind position.

8 Press your outside wheel against the rail to ensure your board stays in grind.

9 Keep your weight over your front foot. Land with your front

The secret to this trick is landing with your nose pressed firmly down on the rail, as well as having your outside front wheel pushed tightly against the rail.

foot on the nose of your board.

10 As you grind the rail, extend your front leg while your back foot is bent, holding you in the krooked grind position.

11 Come off the end of the rail and turn your front foot around slightly and your back foot around so you are straight when you ride away.

Nollie Half Cab Boardslide

1 Ride up with the front of your body facing the rail.

2 Approach at a slight angle or almost parallel to the rail.

3 Place your front foot on the nose and your back foot three inches below the bottom bolts of your back truck. Put your back foot straight across the board, with your toes coming just to the edge.

4 When you are about eight inches from the end of the stairs, pop your nose, slide your back foot up and suck your feet up into your body.

5 Nollie a foot away from the rail.

6 As you ascend into the air, rotate your shoulders 45 degrees and your body will follow.

7 Land with the rail in the middle of your board. Each foot should be covering your truck bolts as you slide.

The secret to this trick is the popping of a nice nollie 180 and landing halfway through it on the rail.

8 As you come off the end of the rail, turn your shoulders and body back so you are facing forward.

9 When you land, bend your knees for absorption.

Frontside 180 Nosegrind

1 Ride up with your back facing the rail.

2 Place your front foot straight across your board and your back foot in the ollie position.

3   Place your front foot three inches below the bottom bolts on your top truck.

4   Approach the rail at a 30 degree angle.

5   Ollie when you near the edge of the stairs.

6 As you ollie, begin rotating your shoulders 180 degrees and bring your body around to follow.

7 As you 180, keep your board level and aim for your front truck to land on the rail after completing the 180.

Frontside 180 Nosegrind

The secret of this trick is to rotate your shoulders enough so you do a complete 180. Also, be sure to keep your weight over your nose as you land in the grind position.

8   As your truck lands on the rail, keep all your weight on your front truck. Both legs should be bent to keep the board in the 180 nosegrind position.

9   As you near the end of the grind, keep your board straight so you are able to ride away.

10   When you land, bend your knees for absorption.

About the author

Evan Goodfellow has been skateboarding since 1988. His sponsers have included Vans Shoes, Ambiguous Clothing, 88 Shoes, Zion Skateboards, and Ninetimes Boardshop. Evan has appeared in eight skate videos and has written three other instructional skateboarding books including *Street Skateboarding: Endless Grinds and Slides, Street Skateboarding: Flip Tricks,* and *Ramp Tricks.* Evan has also written a fictional skateboard book entitled *Skateboard Daze at Hollywood High.*

About the photographer

Tadashi Yamaoda loves to skate and loves shooting skateboard action. For more info and a look at some of his other work, please visit www.tadashiphoto.com

Magazines

The Skateboard Mag
142 N. Cedros Ste. B,
Solana Beach, CA 92075

www.theskateboardmag.com

This magazine was started by former staff members from *Transworld Skateboarding* magazine in an attempt to purify skateboarding from the over-commercialization they felt was taking place at *Transworld Skateboarding*. The quality of the magazine and both the writing and photos make it a top choice among skateboard magazines.

Transworld Skateboarding Magazine
TransWorld Media
353 Airport Rd
Oceanside, CA 92054

www.skateboarding.com

Transworld Skateboarding has been around for a very long time and has always produced good interviews and good photos. The quality of the magazine over the years has helped make it my second choice.

Thrasher Skateboard Magazine
High Speed Productions Inc.
1303 Underwood Ave
San Francisco, CA 94124

www.thrashermagazine.com

Thrasher magazine is based out of San Francisco and often features spots and skateboarders that aren't featured in *Transworld* which brings an added flavor to the skateboard world. This magazine also features cool, up and coming bands, or long established hard core bands.

Color Magazine
Four Corner Publishing Inc.
321 Railway Street
Studio 105
Vancouver, BC
Canada
V6A 1A4

www.colormagazine.ca

This magazine is a new artsy skateboard magazine coming from Canada. It's high quality paper and pictures make it an enjoyable read. The Canadian flavor brings an extra unique taste showing spots and riders that often do not appear in American skateboard magazines.

Skateboard Websites

Ignition Skate
This website was designed for skateboarders to go and check out new videos, post comments and chat with other skateboarders.

www.ignitionsk8.com

Skateboard Village
This website was created for skateboarders to post skate photos, meet other skaters and find out what is new in the world of skateboarding.

www.skateboardvillage.com

Evan's Top 5 Sites

Board Sites

Girl Skateboards
www.girlskateboards.com

Zero Skateboards
www.zeroskateboards.com

Real Skateboards
www.realskateboards.com

Plan B Skateboards
www.planbskateboarding.com

Cliché Skateboards
www.clicheskate.com

Truck Sites

Royal Trucks
www.royalskateboardtruck.com

Independent Trucks
www.independenttrucks.com

Venture Trucks
www.venturetrucks.net

Thunder Trucks
www.thundertrucks.com

Destructo Trucks
www.destructotrucks.com

Shoe Sites

Circa Shoes
www.circafootwear.com

Fallen Shoes
www.fallenfootwear.com

DC Shoes
www.dcshoecousa.com

IPATH Shoes
www.ipath.com

More Skateboard Books from Veva Skateboarding Books

Skateboard Daze at Hollywood High